Dear Grace,
Letters to a
Single Parent

Dear Grace,
Letters to a
Single Parent

Temiika D. Gipson

2010 Copyright © by Temiika D. Gipson

All rights reserved, including the right to reproduce this book or portions thereof in any form by any means—electronic, mechanical, photocopy, recording, or otherwise—without prior written consent of the publisher. For information please address Repairer of the Breach Publications, Attn: Temiika D. Gipson, P.O. BOX 3011, Cordova TN, 38088.

First Printing

Editorial Consultant: Arnita L. Fields

ISBN: 978-0-578-06944-9

All Scripture and references are taken from the New King James Version of the Bible. Copyright © 1985 Thomas Nelson Publishers, Inc. Used by permission. All rights reserved.

Table of Contents

Dedication vii

Acknowledgments ix

Introduction xiii

Letter One   The Divorce 1

Letter Two   Lost in Wrong Relationships 13

Letter Three   A Cry for Help 23

Letter Four   Change Is on the Way 31

Letter Five   My New Life with Christ 37

Letter Six   Hard Times 47

Letter Seven Final Words to Single Parents 59

Letter to the President 63

A Prayer for Single Parents 69

About the Author 71

DEDICATION

To my beautiful children, Arriell, Wendy, Taylor, and Wendell: I love you more than words can ever describe. My life never would have been worth living without the love you've given me. I am thankful that God entrusted me with four precious jewels. It's because of you that I am able to share my joy with the world.

ACKNOWLEDGMENTS

First, giving honor to my Lord and Savior, Jesus. I am so grateful to be a daughter of the King. Thank You so much, God, for Your Spirit and the anointing You have given me. Thank You for Your unconditional and endless love.

To my ex-husband, Wendell, thank you for giving me four beautiful children.

To my mom, Katie, thanks for your love and help. You believed in me when I was at some of the lowest points in my life. Thank you for being a mother and a friend when I needed you.

To Elias Collins, thank you for all the free gas cards, groceries, money, and love. You're the best godfather anyone could ever ask for.

To my sisters, Rheunte and Nina, and my brothers, Fabrice and Baudoin, thank you for being the realest siblings anyone could ever want. Thanks for all the money I "borrowed" and never had to pay back. Nina, thank you for always having my back when I was in need.

To Crystal, thank you! I wouldn't have received a promise of God without your giving heart.

To my best girlfriends, Leslie McClain, Tracye Jones, Katherine Knowles, and Tina Turner, you all are angels on earth sent from heaven. I will never forget your love, kindness, and giving toward me and my children. I love you all very much.

To Michele, thank you for buying my notebook, which enabled me to finish my manuscript.

To momma Lilly, I'm grateful for your encouragements.

To Femi Onafowokan thank you. I pray that these letters will find your friend Grace.

To Dr. Stacy L. Spencer, thank you so much for speaking into my life with discipline, encouragement, and prophecy. Thank you for having a heart of the Father. I love you and First Lady Rhonda, and I am honored to be under your covering.

To Destric Yarbrough, I'm so thankful for the many laughs and your endurance in putting up with my "emotional moments." Thank you for not letting me give in when I so desperately wanted to. When hopelessness came my way, God used you to pick me up. Surely there is a great reward for you! Thanks for being my best male friend when I needed one.

To Antoinette Williams, thanks for encouraging me to share my testimony.

To LeWinfred Shack, thank you so much for your encouragement and for reminding me that it's not about me.

To Arnita Fields, thank you for allowing God to use you in His service. I wouldn't have been able to complete this without you.

Thank you, Angie Kiesling, for your editing skills. Your expert eye helped to make the book the best it can be.

To Pam Minor, God has used you in so many ways to help me. Your prayers have truly blessed me and my children. I will never forget the times you prayed for me at work and during your quiet times.

To all the intercessors who have prayed for me, thank you and I love you.

INTRODUCTION

I became a single parent in April 2000. It has not always been an easy task. During these times there have been many trials and testing of my faith—before I even knew what having real faith was. Many times I thought about giving up on parenting, life, and the responsibility of having to be so strong for my children. Through all the adversities of life, I used the tool of prayer to help me overcome obstacles as I learned to trust God. Prayer helped me to place matters in God's hands, and I've learned to walk my salvation out one day at a time.

As time went by, I grew into the mother God wanted me to be. I am still growing and learning and have a sense of joy while God is yet unfolding His plans. I desired to be complete and to have a loving family, but I never thought I would become a single parent. Even though God did not cause the mishaps, hurt, and pain I experienced in my life, He did step in and turn it all around for my good. God definitely had a different way of bringing me into the maturity of becoming not only a woman of God but also a mother of godly children.

Dear Grace is composed of letters written from the core of my heart to a single parent. I wrote it to target and encourage single parents who struggle with celibacy, parenting, and finding their purpose in life. Before each letter, you will find poems I wrote during my time of worship. It is my prayer that as you are reading, you will be able to walk on your journey more inspired and be ready to conquer all that would come against you in life. My purpose in writing these letters is to inspire, encourage, and uplift every reader who has ever had to face the many challenges I have overcome.

Grace is a person I have never met, but we share a mutual friend. I was told by my friend that Grace is a single parent of three children who needed some encouragement. Because I could not personally contact her I felt that I could help her this way, by sharing my testimony of how God brought me through. Revelation 12:11 states, "We overcome by the Blood of the Lamb and the word of our testimony." This is my testimony, *Dear Grace…*

Watching Me

As I looked up to the sky

I saw Your examining eye

I was so amazed by this brilliant discovery

And so touched to see You watching

It was the most beautiful sight to see

The King of Glory looking at me

Revealing Your presence to those You love

Your eye is brighter than the sunlight's glow

I pondered how this could be

My Lord taking such time to visit me

In all Your duties and Your attention to prayers

You're so amazing to be present everywhere

I'll never forget that day

As I was going about my way

When Your eye appeared to me

Just so I'll know that You see

All of the things I do and say

You're right in my midst every day

Letter One

The Divorce

I lived with my ex-husband for about eight years. Some of those years were good but most of them were very dysfunctional. We met when I was eighteen years old while I was taking some classes at a nearby college. Shortly thereafter (within three months) I was pregnant with our first child. We didn't have much of a relationship even then because it was mostly a sexual relationship. And since we didn't really date we never had the opportunity to become friends before we were married. I'm getting ahead of myself right now, so I will talk about this situation a little bit later.

During the pregnancy we went our separate ways. His brother was killed in a freak accident, and he was going through all sorts of emotions and didn't want me to have the baby. Two months before our daughter was born, we started having more conversations and he convinced me that he wanted a relationship. After our daughter was born, I moved in with him and his parents.

Things were difficult for me because I had become very dependent upon his family and grew further away from my own. My mother wasn't in agreement with me living with him, but I didn't want to stay home either. I suppose you could say I actually wanted to be a part of what people might say is a "normal" family. He and I soon found ourselves part of a dysfunctional relationship where I had to deal with both physical and emotional abuse.

He was this gorgeous man who seemed to have everything together, and he was a free spender. He had dated some of the prettiest women, so because of this I felt as if I was never good enough or pretty enough for him. I was very insecure in our relationship and I did not know my self-worth. I felt lucky to have someone like him in my life, but the emotional abuse I endured throughout our relationship damaged my soul. Not only did I feel like I wasn't good enough, he constantly reminded me of it. I was very submissive then; I did what I knew to do as a live-in girlfriend, although I never learned to cook much. I most definitely didn't keep my house as neat and clean as his mother once we moved out into our own home, but I tried. It really didn't matter much because nothing would have made him love me the way I needed to be loved. I was only nineteen years old, and he was about five years older. We couldn't have possibly known what true love was anyway at that age.

We got married close to three years later, only because I was pregnant again and we wanted to do what seemed to be the right thing to do at the time. It wasn't a great feeling to be living with someone and unmarried. I wanted to feel appreciated so much, and I wanted to be loved. I desired to have a real family, but little did I know getting married wasn't going to make things any better.

During our marriage we argued and we had sex. He worked most of the day so I only saw him in the mornings and late evenings. I don't believe we really knew what it meant to be married. I most certainly wasn't prepared for what I had gotten myself into. I wasn't raised in a way that prepared me to be a wife at that age. I believe at some point I wanted to love him but didn't know how.

The household I came from did not exemplify the characteristics of a loving marriage. My dad never married my mom, and when my mom did get married, my stepfather wasn't the "take on the stepchildren as my own" type. During childhood every girl has a vision in her heart of what she wants her marriage to be like. Well, at least I did. Somehow I felt I got the short end of the stick and was forced to grow up faster than I should have.

I became pregnant again a couple of years later, and I remember being so miserable during my pregnancy. We had already been considering a divorce prior to the pregnancy, and we were having a lot of difficulties in our marriage. My husband confessed to me about having an affair, and I couldn't move forward because of the thoughts of betrayal in addition to the emotional abuse. I wanted out of what had now become a mess. When I discovered I was pregnant, I was somewhat sad from knowing we were not getting along well, and I could imagine how much harder things would get. This was an interesting insight to me since we had apparently been getting along well enough to conceive our children. But as I said before, that was all our marriage consisted of: sex and fighting.

When I found out later that I was having twins, I sank into a depression and couldn't believe I was pregnant with two babies at once. In addition to my concern about carrying twins, I also could not remember the time of their conception. So in light of this I felt the most logical thing for me to do at that time was to just make it work because I had now become the mother of four children. This along with not making a lot of money seemed like reason enough to stay in a relationship that would soon seek to destroy me.

Things became worse as we grew further apart. Our marriage had no meaning at this point, and because there had been marital unfaithfulness, misunderstandings, and confusion in the midst of it all, I didn't have much hope to hold onto. When I decided to file for a divorce a year and a half later, I remained living in the same house with him. I felt as if I had nowhere else to go, and he didn't want to leave because it was a house that he had inherited. I chose to stay. I did not want to go back to my family at the time because of the shame and guilt from my failures.

It soon became extremely hard to live under the same roof. About one month after I filed for divorce, we were in a really bad fight that resulted in his attempt to kill me. I should have known it would be dangerous to stay there from the previous physical altercations. One night while I was preparing dinner he came into the kitchen and put a belt around my neck, nearly choking me. I had been holding a plate in my hand and dropped it on the floor. He just laughed as I cleaned up the broken glass.

Then something even more horrible happened on the last night that I lived in our home. I will never forget that night even though I have since received great healing in this area. It was about 2 a.m. when he came home. I was asleep, and when he came into the bedroom where I was sleeping he grabbed me by my feet and pulled me out of the bed and down through the halls. I desperately tried to hold onto the corners of the doorway. He was much stronger than I was and every attempt I made to hold onto the door failed. Finally, after much struggle, he dragged me through the living room and out the front door.

I can remember looking back seeing my children screaming and crying out. I don't think they even knew what was really going on at the time. He pulled me up to a glass end-table that was on the porch. He grabbed a brick and held it over my head. I still have a mental picture of that brick as I am writing to you, Grace. I remember seeing the anger in his face as he held the brick up in his hand. And then there it was, the moment I thought I was going to meet death face-to-face. I heard him say the unthinkable: "It's too late now. You have got to die now b----!" I closed my eyes and began to recite part of the Lord's Prayer: "Our Father, which art in heaven, hallowed be Thy name. Thy Kingdom come, Thy will be done, on earth as it is in heaven…" I remember saying it over about three times.

Suddenly he dropped the brick, and I somehow got away from him, ran into the house, grabbed my keys and my babies, and made a dash to my minivan. As I tried to get away, he came after me in his truck and even tried to run me off the road. I dialed 911 and screamed into my cell phone pleading for help. Soon I pulled up to a fire station and started blasting the horn so someone would come out of the station to help me. As this was happening he left, and soon after the police showed up.

No arrest was made. The policewoman told me that since I didn't have any visible bruises, except for the one on my thumb from holding onto the corners of the doorway, no evidence of abuse would show up on a camera. She told me I could file a report with the citizen dispute department, but I didn't think they would do anything either. Besides,

I worked at the Criminal Justice Center! I knew how the system worked when there was a lack of proof. I left the fire station early that Thursday morning and went to my sister's home. It had to be about four in the morning. I was very scared, confused, and hopeless. I was also in shock.

Days later I went to apply for an apartment, but at that time my credit was horrible. Everything I owned was in my name, and I had become delinquent on the payments, but a property manager at this complex was, I believe, truly sent by God. I told her about my situation and how I had four children with nowhere to go. She put me up in an apartment two days later. I called on friends to help me pay the deposit and first month's rent. I also called my dad and my brothers to help me, and they met me at my former home to help pack up my things. I was then able to move into a two-bedroom townhouse.

My dad was very sad about the whole ordeal. He said he wished he had known about my living circumstances. Honestly, none of my family knew about the abuse. I never told them about how miserable I was. I didn't ask them for help because I felt I was in that thing on my own. Thankfully I was able to escape that lifestyle. I had reached a point in my life where I was given another chance. I now had a chance to allow God to show me a better way. This was all by the grace of God, although I didn't realize it at the time. I was used to talking with God but didn't really have a relationship with Him. Unbeknownst to me, our relationship would soon be formed, but I will discuss more of this with you later, Grace.

My move signaled the beginning of my journey as a single woman and single parent. I was about twenty-six years old at this time.

I can remember talking to a friend about my situation before I actually filed for divorce. I told him I was so afraid of moving out on my own and that I didn't know how I could make it without my husband's help. My friend told me, "Temiika, you're already doing it by yourself." That was an eye-opener, and when it became just the five of us I felt I could raise my children on my own. My friend was a fireman, and I suppose that's why I drove to a fire station the night my ex-husband tried to run me off the road. I went to the place that signified hope. Looking back while writing this is remarkable because I still don't know how some needs were met, but they were. God was there all along and guiding me even when I didn't realize it.

Months after my separation my minivan was repossessed. I was devastated. I didn't have a car to get to work and I didn't have extra money to purchase another one. I didn't know what I was going to do. Well, let's just back up a little bit. Of course I didn't have money to purchase another vehicle because I couldn't even pay the note on the one I had! It was the most horrible feeling not to know how things would work out. But once again God intervened and blessed me. He always made a way for me, even when I didn't acknowledge Him. My ex-husband's parents ended up giving me one of their cars. They wanted to make sure the children were cared for, and so they provided the means for my travel. I was very grateful to have transportation. The back windows were disabled and couldn't go down, and the car didn't have air conditioning, but I was very happy to have a way to work.

Seven months passed and my divorce became final. I didn't want anything except for him to pay child support for the care of the children. But oh was that a BIG mistake. I regretted that decision big-time. To this day, Grace, I can't believe I agreed to receive $800 monthly for four children. What was I thinking? I guess when you have dealt with as much as I had, you only want what's needed to get by. I wish I had made better decisions concerning the child support. It was so hard for me to raise my children the way I wanted to with that amount. I wish I had finished school and had a better paying job so I didn't have to depend on child support as much. My children deserved the best in life, simply because they were my babies.

Sometimes after a long day of working, I would drive home wondering what we would eat and how I was going to take care of our needs. Raising my children was very difficult for me, but I always wanted the best for them. They didn't have to know we were poor. They didn't have to know I cried myself to sleep wondering what I was going to do. They didn't have to know I was depressed. They just had to know that I loved them so much and would do anything to give them the best of what I had to offer, even in my lack. The more I talked to God about my circumstances, the more things would get easier for me.

Questions to Ponder

What was your relationship like with the father or mother of your children?

How did you feel when that relationship ended?

What effects has the separation or divorce had on your living arrangements?

Have you been able to forgive the father or mother of your children?

Have you been able to forgive yourself?

Hold Me

Hold Me in your arms
Never let Me go
I'll wipe away your fears
And you'll always know I'm near

Hold Me in your arms
Never let Me go
Watch your cares fade today
And learn to see things My way

Hold Me in your arms
Never let Me go
My virtue will be imparted
And your mistakes are discarded

Hold Me in your arms
Never let Me go
Where my protection is limitless
And where my love brings you rest

Hold Me in your arms
Never let Me go
You can hide under My shadow
And worship Me as if there's no tomorrow

Hold Me in your arms
Never let Me go

So we can become one

Just as the Father, Holy Spirit, and Son

Hold Me in your arms

Never let Me go

Birth the joy that springs from above

As I descend upon you as a dove

Hold Me in your arms

Never let Me go

I will put in your spirit a new song

It shall be called the Song of the Lord

Letter Two

Lost in Wrong Relationships

My goodness, where do I begin! There came a time in my life when I was involved with people I should never have been dealing with. I was free from my ex-husband but still bound by the emotional abuse. A seed of discouragement was planted after my divorce from my ex-husband and his dad. His dad told me that if I found a man who would want to marry me with four children, he would kiss his behind (respectfully stated). My ex-husband told me I would never marry again and especially with four children. He told me I would just be a good sex partner (and that's saying it nicely). So of course that was the very thing that drove me to seek for some kind of comfort.

On one hand I wanted to prove them wrong, and on the other I had accepted my status and lived out the words that were spoken over me. For two and a half years I was on this rebellious sex spree, searching for love or acceptance that I could never receive from these men. Each relationship provided a pervasive misperception of what unconditional love really was. Because they were not based on what God wanted them to be, perversion and deception had their way.

I've wondered why such desperation would cause us as human beings to run into the arms or beds of others when all we need to do is surrender to the Lord, but surely that was the last thing on my mind. I didn't know at the time it was God's love I needed. I just knew I felt so empty inside. No one could help me and no one could please me. As far as I was concerned, I could never be complete after all I suffered. I didn't feel attractive, I didn't feel that I was good enough to be someone's wife, I didn't feel that I was worth someone falling in love with me, and I most certainly didn't feel that I deserved better.

It's interesting how the enemy will use people to try to plant lies in our minds. I was wounded and lost in a field of insecurity, but one thing I can say is that through all of this I always talked to God. Though it might sound strange to say that, it is true. I was living a lifestyle of heavy sin and yet still talking to God. It wasn't a method of prayer or anything eloquent, I just talked to God the way I'm writing to you, Grace, from the heart. It was as if I knew my outcome would be greater than what I was experiencing at the time. It seemed as if I was watching my life from up above the whole time. I used to tell people I felt like I had been asleep during those times, and then later suddenly awakened and made alive, living for Christ.

Looking back in time, I was so lonely. I didn't know how in the world I would make it through. I believe I turned to forbidden relationships as a substitute for love. I always longed for love even while I was married. I wondered if I always lived in a world of fantasy and fairytale as I thought back on the dreams I had of what a marriage should be. I knew couples who always appeared happy in their relationships, and I would say I wish I had what they had. Grace, I probably did have what they had, dysfunction! Not everything is as it seems. Unless you truly know what takes place in a person's home, you only see what they allow you to see. Single parents are quick to compare themselves with the appearance of another's lifestyle.

Getting back to wrong relationships, what makes relationships wrong? I suppose it would be those relationships that you know you have absolutely no business being involved in, especially if you or the other person is married. This is not the same as having a very good friend who just happens to be married where there is a pure friendship. I am talking about getting intimately involved with a married person. Intimacy is not the same as sexual intercourse. Intimacy is more detailed and deeply attached.

When you find yourself talking to a married person for hours in a day, sending thoughtful text messages, flirting, sharing intimate desires for each other, and then telling the person that you are in love with them, it will usually form an emotional bond by itself. Ungodly soul ties are formed when there is an exchange of impure motives. When you emotionally give of yourself to another person in a way that is not intended for you, then you have allowed a place in your heart for someone who doesn't belong there. This place is supposed to be reserved only for your spouse, but I didn't care. My marriage had failed and because I wasn't healed from my brokenness, I didn't have respect for the marriages of the men who were interested in me.

I actually had no problem getting in these wrong relationships and didn't know how it happened at times. I never went out looking for anyone but always attracted the wrong people. I guess that says a lot about the men I was dealing with then. If the truth be told, they were probably just as messed up on the inside as I was. I allowed myself to be so degraded, Grace, and when I didn't have my way,

I would manipulate and lie for sympathy. I'm sure I somehow made them feel that they were someone special in my life because I was very good at listening to problems and even appeared to care. Those kinds of mind games were strictly from the soul. I had too many emotions working against me and didn't know how to cut off the relationships or the behavior. I'm sure there is a psychological term for this. Needless to say, I was in bondage.

I eventually got to the point where I would become dependent on men to provide for me. I would accept money from those I was sexually involved with. A couple of the men I was seeing (on separate time frames) were professional athletes. Both were married, but my mindset was all about trying to support my family. So while trying to make ends meet and to justify my wrong thinking, I would sometimes say to myself that I was a divorced parent with four children and barely receiving enough in child support to make what I was doing okay. In these relationships there were some men I just wanted to spend time with and others whom I used to my advantage.

One day I met a guy who captured my heart in a different way than the others. I didn't know how to love him, and we did not have much of a relationship, but I liked him very much. We were connected emotionally, and I'm sure it was an ungodly soul tie, but neither of us was living a lifestyle that reflected a Christlike image. I don't think he cared about a Christlike image as much as I did either. I was easy, and I'm sure he enjoyed what was given to him so freely. We messed around for a little over a year. I had begun to fall in love with him but knew that he wasn't interested in a real relationship. I really liked spending time with him, and he came over at least three nights a week.

He would never stay over the entire night but came for what he wanted and then left. I used to ask him to spend the night but he would not. He told me that spending the night would confuse the matter. At this point I can't explain the reasoning behind the delusion, and once again I was left hurt and rejected.

He made it very clear what he wanted from the beginning, what he wanted from me. What is it with men who say "I don't want to be in a committed relationship" but still engage in "committed relationship" activity? Is their honesty supposed to make women trust them more or challenge them? Oftentimes women want the very things they cannot or should not have, and they end up driven by a desire that they either execute on the goal of obtaining or decide to give up. I'm not sure what I was thinking, but for whatever reason in my confused mind I fell for it. Grace, I wish I had an ounce of the confidence back then that I have today.

One thing I can say is that although I was lost in so many wrong relationships, I never brought any of the men around my children, and this is why I only saw them at night. My children were usually asleep before I would have any company. I didn't want my children to know this side of me, plus I was working in a place where I saw the convictions of all sorts of crime such as the rape of a child from the victim's stepdads, uncles, or mother's boyfriends. Thank God I had enough sense to keep my children away from those men. Grace, I really don't remember any of them wanting to be a part of my children's life anyway. They were only in my life for pleasure and not for true love.

I soon grew tired of being hurt and let down, but little did I know that a change was soon coming my way. And you know what, Grace? I was tired of the whole pretense too. Despite how lonely I felt, I wanted God to help me so badly. I can remember praying about the emptiness and asking God to take it away.

Questions to Ponder

Do you know your self-worth?

Are you willing to receive God's love for you?

Are you in a relationship that God would approve of?

Is it a healthy relationship?

If not, what adjustments can be made to make your relationship healthy?

Tears in God's Bottle

Put my tears into Your bottle
So they will no longer rest
in their pool of sorrow

Number and name them
for Your safekeeping
Even the ones that fell
while I was sleeping

Take a written account
of what caused them to form
And place their prayer requests
in a special barn of its own

Put my tears into Your bottle
From the core of my soul
they have burst through

Gather them to ferment
for a priceless use
Especially those that have
been poured out on You

This waterfall of concern,
love and happiness
Handle them one by one
Until Your purpose of
their creation has come

Put my tears into Your bottle
Hold it gently and close
to Your loving heart
Protect the glass that keeps them
never to break apart

Know the meaning of their being
and how precious is the heart
they were birthed from
Help them to feel no pain and
let the harvest of their joy come

Letter Three

A Cry for Help

It was nearly three years after my divorce, and by then I was worn out by my lifestyle. I was depressed and didn't want to work. I didn't want to raise my children alone anymore either. I felt like I had nowhere to turn and no one to turn to. One of my best girlfriends told me she had put me on the prayer list at her church because she was very concerned about me. My friend and I were so different from each other. She belonged to the Church of Christ denomination and is very reserved and quiet-tempered.

I knew she loved me and my children, and I never questioned her motives. She often volunteered to babysit, but I felt that they would be a burden so I kept them close to me and would not let other people watch them. She had to be heaven-sent into my life, especially with her gifts of expensive clothes, suits, and shoes, some of which had never been worn and still had the tags on them. She always made sure I was taken care of. She offered money and helped as if she were my biological sister. With all those acts of kindness, I still never let her take the children off my hands so that I could have time to myself as she suggested.

Many experiences from my life played a part in why I shielded my children in the manner I did. My experience at the age of five when I felt abandoned after my mom married my stepfather and moved to Tahiti may have played a part. My older sister and I stayed behind for a short time with my grandmother, and before we joined my mother we lived with friends of hers and my stepfather's in New Zealand. I missed my mom a lot, and my dad wasn't around much. I don't think we realize the pain children experience when there is a disconnection in the family. Whether it's a physical separation or emotional one, something has to replace the void that's left on the inside of you. So I always kept my children close to me because I didn't want them to feel the same kind of abandonment I felt. Even though I was later reunited with my mom, living without her for that short period of time left a wound.

My ex-husband always had a way of reminding me that I would not succeed in life. I never felt I was good enough to do anything after talking to him, feeding my already low self-esteem. Even though he had agreed to pay me child support I didn't get the money unless I begged for it, and I had to call him weekly asking for the money. At this time I didn't have it set up with the courts to receive my child support payments, so I had to depend on him for things even after we were divorced. It was such an issue of control, it seemed as though he wanted me to always need him.

It was getting harder to care for my children. Money was low so I applied for government assistance but was denied. They said I wasn't in the bracket of need according to my income and the size of my family. They obviously didn't understand how difficult it was to support a family of five on a fixed income. I bet some of the families who received assistance were living better than we were. They didn't have to worry about bills and food, or worry about keeping shelter for their family. I don't think they even had to worry about paying for daycare expenses. Child care and after-school care were very expensive. Grace, I believe I might still owe somebody for child care today! The staffs were understanding at some centers and forgave the amount due while another made attempts to sue me for the balance. I paid it to prevent my wages from being garnished.

As time passed, I searched for a new place to live because we needed more space. My children were all in the same bedroom and sharing beds. I've always been grateful for God placing us in that apartment complex. It was good for a while, but something in me always wanted better for us. Eventually we moved into a house I rented from one of the judge's secretaries, although the rent was more than what I could afford. It did not matter to me; I just wanted to give my children the best, and I wanted to live in an environment where the school systems were better.

I found the house not far from where I had lived before I got married. The rent, $800, was the same amount I was receiving in child support payments. I didn't know how in the world I was going to pull it all together, but I was just happy to be there. We had more space and the children could go outside and play in a safe environment. We had a fenced-in backyard and also an extra bathroom and bedroom. This was so much better than the five of us living in a two-bedroom townhouse.

Soon I started to feel the weight of what I had just entered into. I didn't fully understand that the choice I made was going to be a huge burden on me. I could barely make ends meet when I was in the two-bedroom townhouse, so I don't know why I thought paying nearly $300 more a month in rent would be any better. The rent was more, the utilities were more, and it even seemed like the cost of food was more expensive too. I wasn't seeing the other men as much anymore so I couldn't get money from them as I did before. I was tired of the game and tired of longing for something unreachable. More importantly, I was tired of hurting and gradually drifted from most of the wrong relationships.

I remember crying to God for help one evening after my children's dad had come over to pick them up. We had gotten into a huge argument over financial responsibility, and after he left I started talking to God. I told God I didn't want to live anymore. I know this was a very bad state of mind to be in, and I knew I didn't want to leave my children behind either. I would ask God to just take us all together. I didn't care how He did it, I just wanted to go. I was never bold enough to harm myself or the children; I was just hurt and wanted to give up. But God would not allow it, Grace, because He knew I was quickly approaching breakthrough. That night I went to bed with a peaceful heart. It seemed as if my cares were temporarily taken away.

In the meantime, I was beginning to get more focused on the emotional stability of my children. My oldest daughter was a great helper around the house, and she had a lot of responsibilities. I was so caught up in the lack of things and myself that I neglected to make sure I was being a good parent. Life was happening so fast for me and was pretty much routine. I realized I wasn't there for my kids in the way they needed me to be. I made sure they had the necessary care, but I don't think I provided the closeness they wanted and deserved. I cried out to God and asked Him to help me be a better parent.

My children needed a love that wasn't available to them because of the deep void I had and my own emotional instability. I wanted to love them the way every child should be loved. I just didn't really know how to, Grace. Don't misunderstand me, they were happy children and well cared for, but they should have gotten more hugs and kisses from me. I should have told them I loved them more often, and I should have spent more time watching them smile or listening to their conversations as I do today.

Shortly after this, my life began to change. I told my friends that in the coming year I was going to start "living right" and be celibate. They laughed at me, and I probably laughed with them. I just knew I wanted to start living a different lifestyle. I even started reading the Bible. Psalm 23 was the only Scripture passage I would turn to during this time because it was the only thing I understood while reading my Bible. I had the King James Version then and didn't understand the meaning or the terminology of the Scriptures, but Psalm 23 was a passage I would recite over and over again.

The New Year was approaching and I continued telling people that I was going to change my way of living. Even after the New Year came I was still involved in sexual sin. In the back of my mind I knew I would have to give up having sex. I remember telling the guy I fell in love with that he should enjoy me then because I wasn't going to be doing it much longer. Interestingly enough, he finally decided to spend the night with me. I was blown away by that. I always longed to know what it would be like for him to hold me through the night. I asked him constantly if he had to go but he said he was fine with staying over. However, I was convinced that it was our last time together like this.

I knew I wasn't going to be sexually active with him anymore. I didn't know I was speaking into my own life, and I didn't know how it was going to happen, but something deep inside let me know I would soon be living a lifestyle free from sexual bondage.

In the past I was so bound to sexual sins. I was heavily active in stimulating my body. At times even when driving my car I would think of the need to be filled in this area. It was always a desire for me, and I didn't care how I would get it done just as long as that mission was accomplished. This wasn't something that came about after I was divorced but started early in my life as a preteen. After my divorce it just manifested fully. However deep the bondage was, I still knew in my heart that I was coming out of it and I wasn't going to let that hope go. I had determined in my heart to see myself free.

Questions to Ponder

Do you believe God will answer your cry for help?

How often do you communicate with God?

Do you want to be set free from bondage?

Are you taking the necessary steps towards freedom?

Song of the Lord

Your breath upon my face
Whispering Your desires
My heart feels Your embrace
Your Spirit takes me higher

Lord I want to be Yours
Lord take me into doors
Lord guide me in this place
Release Your great grace

Letter Four

Change Is on the Way

In the early months of that New Year, I had a strong urge to go back to church. I visited a church that one of my friends attended. He and his wife were active members, and he had invited me one Sunday morning. He would always tell people about how the Lord was moving in a powerful way at the church. When I went to check it out, my children and I sat in the back row of the church, and during the worship service we stood and clapped as the choir sang. At some point between the praise songs, I suppose it was routine for the congregation to just break free. They would get excited in the Spirit and run as the Holy Spirit led them. Grace, I didn't even know who the Holy Spirit was then. I knew about God and I knew His Son Jesus, but that summed up my knowledge of God back then.

    I don't think I had ever witnessed a day such as this one. I watched as my friend's wife ran a lap around the church in excitement. During the second lap, she ran toward me and grabbed my hand! And there we went, running laps around the church sanctuary. I had absolutely no clue as to what I was doing. I just smiled as I held onto her hand. I then caught a glimpse of my children laughing at me. My son laughed so hard he fell out of his chair; he was about four years old then.

Needless to say, I knew in my heart that God was heavily involved in what she did. After the holy workout I went back to my seat, and if I remember correctly my children were amazed and still laughing. Little did we know that laughing is a weapon of warfare. Of course I had no idea what weapons of warfare were back then, but I'm just thinking "out loud" right now, Grace. After the service she told me the Holy Spirit told her to grab my hand while she was running. She said she didn't know why or what it was for, but out of obedience she took me along. I didn't feel any different in the natural after that day. I also didn't return to that church for a while!

Although I didn't feel any different, unique encounters happened to me that same week. I was at work one day and a friend and I were talking by the elevator. Out of nowhere this lady came up to us saying we had better get our lives right with God and that there were two important dates in our lives, a birth date and a death date, and we don't have any control over when each one happens. After she left us we laughed. I told my friend that word of warning was for him, and he said his pastor—who is now my apostle—taught them that if you think a word is for someone else it's usually for you. I didn't understand why I had this encounter, but I just went on my way after it occurred.

A couple of weeks later I attended this big concert with my friends, and we were having a great time. After the concert we went to an after-party at a local nightclub. We stayed out very late, probably until about 3 a.m. By this time I was ready to go because I wanted to go to church the next morning. I went to my mom's house first to pick up my children. She was angry with me because she didn't want me waking them up and taking them out at that time of the morning. She didn't understand that the scar I had from my childhood was still fresh and I didn't want to leave them overnight.

That next morning as I was trying to figure out which church to attend, I wanted to go desperately but did not return to the one I had visited a couple of weeks before. Many of my other friends attended another church called New Direction Christian Church, so I decided to visit there. As I was driving to church that day I heard deep within me a thought stating that a certain song would be sung at the church I would belong to. I thought it strange that I was having these thoughts, not to mention that I was listening to that same song on the radio while on the way to church.

During the worship time the choir sang that very song! I was shocked. I was not aware of how God could allow things like this to take place. I couldn't believe I was hearing them sing the same song I thought of and heard while in the car. The message was even better; the pastor seemed to be preaching out of the book of the life of Temiika. He talked about those who were at the concert the night before and how we were living dangerously. He talked about the hopelessness and the desire for God to change the way we lived. He talked about choosing Christ and how Jesus would set us free from sin and bondage.

Everything I had experienced up to that moment seemed to be spoken in that message. When it was time for an invitation to join the church I sat still in my seat. I knew that I belonged there but sat frozen in fear. There was too much happening that resonated with my life. Grace, I thought, how could this be? How could someone know so much about what you're going through and where you've been? How could this preacher say all these things that had everything to do with my life in one moment? I was so amazed but I did not join the church that day. I know now that it was the Holy Spirit speaking through my apostle. I am so thankful that God sent me to that place at the right time of my life.

Questions to Ponder

What does change mean to you?

Are you ready for Change?

Are you willing to surrender your entire life to Christ?

What actions can you take to embrace change?

Are you willing to completely yield to God's correction?

Gathering of My Sheep

Once planted and full of nurturing light
But then encountered a moment of strife
And you wandered across mountains and hills
But know My child it was not My will
For you to lack the shepherd you needed
But they disobeyed me and became conceited

Now is the time for you to be gathered
To a safe place of a righteous father
He is one who is after My own heart
This is a place where I have marked
As a field of gardens all about
For you to rest in glory My child

So come along with Me and see
As My outstretched arms embrace thee
To wash away the hurts of the past
That once had a hold on you but didn't last
Know that My love for you is immeasurable
And you're now in a season of the incredible

Letter Five

My New Life with Christ

The following week I went back to the same church, and at the invitation to join I started feeling really nervous. I knew I was supposed to join, but somehow fear came upon me again. My friend looked at me and said she wanted to join. I said, "Me too!" So I went up to the altar and rededicated my life to Christ and made this church my new home.

I was so excited for my children and me. I knew in my heart that God would be a Father to us all and He would help us. I had such peace about the decision I had made for my family. I soon became very sensitive to things relating to Christianity. I can remember crying about the fact that there were not many Christian commercials on TV. I truly wanted everyone to know about the peace and love I had in my heart. God began speaking to me through the Scriptures as well. I opened my Bible one night and a piece of paper fell out with Matthew 5:6 written on it. I went to that verse, and it read, "Blessed are those who hunger and thirst for righteousness, for they shall be filled." I did not have a clue what God was trying to tell me, but I liked it and I liked the fact that I could be blessed.

My children definitely benefited from my new life in Christ. I began to see them in a different light. I no longer regarded them as a burden; now they had become an honor for me. When I saw the characteristics of their dad within them and smiled, I told God that I would embrace those memories and it would be like loving my ex-husband from a distance.

Many things happened very quickly with my spiritual life. It was as if I had been asleep for twenty-nine years and suddenly awakened. My perspective of nearly everything in life had changed. I know you have heard stories about people seemingly changing overnight, and this is the best way I can describe it to you. I was awakened to a newness that only God could create. I thought about all the sinful things I did and felt so guilty and shameful. Of course I know God didn't bring those emotions upon me, but I was the type of person who would ask myself, "How could you have done such things?"

My children and I were growing closer. I always had a strong bond with them, but in this closeness I was paying better attention to their needs and what they wanted from me. It seemed like they were growing up so fast. I actually took time out just to watch their actions and understand their thought patterns. There was never a dull moment in my house. I still laugh at the stories my children tell of things they did while I was working or even during the summer months. My children have always been very close to each other. The younger ones are really close to my oldest daughter because she was there for them in a way that I wasn't when I was going through the trials of life. Instead of coming into my bedroom in the middle of the night because something frightened them, they would go to my oldest daughter's bed.

One day at a time I came to know God more intimately. I couldn't wait to get home from work so I could meet with Him in my prayer closet. These were the most beautiful encounters. Even as I am typing here on my notebook, I'm thinking, "Gosh, why did I stop running to the prayer closet after I got home from work!" Needless to say, spending time with God is priceless. It doesn't have to happen in a certain place; you can spend time with God anywhere. That's because His Spirit lives inside of you. Now I find myself praying or communicating with God while driving, bathing, and even while cleaning. I am now very aware of His presence! Even if I don't "feel" Him near, I know He is always there. It makes me smile just thinking about it.

God also was using me to encourage others. He would send people across my path who had experiences similar to what I had just overcome. It was so magical to me in the beginning. But while it was an honor, it was very surprising as well because I didn't think I qualified to share the goodness of God. I had always communicated with God as a child but didn't know Him in the way that I did by this time.

When I was younger I used to tell my mom I thought I was psychic because I could always sense when something was about to happen, and I always had dreams about events that seemed to take place. Today I know that it was my prophetic nature, but because I had no knowledge of the gifts of the Spirit, I just thought as most people do who are unaware of God's Spirit activated on the inside of them. It's so amazing how when God places His gifts inside of you, they will still operate even without the understanding that it is His Spirit enabling you to be used by Him in such a manner. I'm thankful now that I know more about who I am so that I can let Him use me more. It's all for His glory!

I was experiencing the most unusual amount of favor from people. They would call me up or come to me saying God had placed it on their hearts to give me things like money, clothes, and even paying bills! One of my best girlfriends told me God directed her to pay my cell phone bill. I was extremely grateful, Grace. That was about $50 a month that I didn't have to worry about. And you know what? She still pays that very same cell phone bill today, five years later!

It was only a matter of time until I came into the knowledge that God had a call on my life. He started sending more people along the way, and I would always encourage them. I started praying for people more and just praying for things in general that had absolutely nothing to do with me personally. God would place it in my heart to read certain scriptures about prophecy and prophets, but I didn't understand them. The Bible seemed like it was written in Greek to me at the time. I kept asking God, "What does prophecy mean, and what in the world is a prophet?" It was quite frustrating. I actually looked up the definitions in a dictionary.

One thing about me for sure is that I will seek out what I need to know! I love to research things, so every time God would reveal something new I would find the meaning of it. I was so intrigued by these scriptures that always seemed to pop up in my mind. One in particular was Jeremiah 1:5, which reads, "Before I formed you in the womb I knew you; before you were born I sanctified you; and I ordained you a prophet to the nations." By then you would think I got the picture and could comprehend what God was relating, but it wasn't clear to me yet.

Soon people started confirming what God was communicating to me. I still didn't really believe it though. They would say things like, "Temiika, there is a call on your life," or they would tell me that the things I shared with them happened shortly after I told them. This was all new to me so I would smile and not comment on any of it. One day while I was sleeping I was awakened by the audible voice of God. It was the most amazing encounter I've ever had. His voice was thunderous and distinctive. It was so clear, and although it was very deep, I was surrounded by the most beautiful peace.

As I opened my eyes from sleeping, He asked, "My child, why do you have doubt?" By this time I was in complete shock. I can't remember to this day the rest of what He spoke to me, but I do know He was confirming the plans and purpose He had for my life. He had an expected end to all the things I had experienced in my life, as well as to what I would encounter leading to the time I am reunited with Him in heaven. Jeremiah 29:11 states, "For I know the thoughts that I think toward you, says the Lord, thoughts of peace and not evil, to give you a future and a hope." God already had it in His plans to bless me. I just needed to surrender to His way and the life He wanted me to live.

After all I had just experienced with God, I still sent my pastor an email and had the nerve to ask, "How do you know when you've been called to ministry?" I didn't get a response to my email, but the next Sunday at church there was an announcement stating that if you felt like God was calling you to ministry, you could attend an orientation for a Student Ministers class. I was again amazed at how God was leading me along the path He had designed for me.

I attended Bible study every week and was growing closer to God daily. One day my pastor had an altar call, and although I wanted to go up for prayer I was afraid to go to the altar. Suddenly I jumped out of my seat! I have no idea what came over me, but it was as if someone pushed me or pulled me forward. Whatever it was, it didn't work because I ran to the restroom instead. I was so nervous, but at the same time I knew I needed to be at that altar. I finally came to my senses, left the restroom, and went to the altar for prayer. He prayed for me and I felt something different inside immediately. I can't describe the feeling but I knew something was different on the inside of me.

As I was driving home, I started crying and stretching my hand out toward the cars, praying for the drivers. I was so emotional that I had to pull over on the side of the road. I told God that I didn't want to live my life as I did before. And I also told God I wanted to be clean and free from sexual sin and sexual desires. I told Him that I didn't want to feel the dirt and pain and asked Him to take it all away. Since then I have been celibate. I stopped talking to men on the phone, and I didn't even let them come over to my home. I stopped drinking alcoholic beverages. All of this from just one touch from my pastor's hand and a prayer. I can tell you right now, Grace, that the touch I felt was from God, and I was on my way to discovering more about life with Him.

Although I was excited about my new life with Christ, my journey to discovering who I was in Christ was not the best experience. While I had an extreme zeal to know what God was doing in me, I was also coming against a lot of opposition. My goodness, no one ever told me about warfare and church hurt, but I will save those details for my next book to you, Grace, sharing my call to ministry with letters to prophets. I did make a joke recently that I would write about the one million plus one reasons why I wanted to quit church. Let's just say there is no hurt like church hurt.

Nevertheless, I am still in the race and don't plan on retreating to the enemy at all. God's grace has brought me through it all, and I am thankful for the healing that has taken place. God's love will cause you to forgive anything and anyone. It was just harder on me because I had come out of so much dysfunction and rejection from looking for love, then coming into the church only to experience dysfunction and rejection from those who were supposed to do nothing more than love and nurture me.

One thing I learned was that because I was bound in rejection before I gave my entire heart to Christ, the enemy always tried to use rejection to destroy me. But God would always step in to stop the enemy's plans. I belonged to God and I would never give up on His love. I love Him so much for bringing me out of what I experienced, and I trust Him because of the love He showed to me. I was now able to hold onto His promises because I experienced His love one- on-one.

There was another scripture God always placed on my heart. It was Matthew 6:33: "But seek first the Kingdom of God and His righteousness, and all these things shall be added to you." This sent me on a journey of seeking out the meaning of what God was promising me. I knew He wanted me to have His righteousness from the first message He gave me through the Scriptures. I was on a search to find out what the kingdom of God was and how I could obtain it.

In the verses before Matthew 6:33, Jesus talks about not worrying about your life, food, and clothes. He talks about feeding the birds and how God clothes the grass of the field and knows that we need the things stated (Matthew 6:25-32). I was drawn into the words of Jesus. I wanted this promise for me and my children. I never wanted to depend on another man for anything else; I had a Father in heaven who was willing to provide for me for FREE. All I needed to do was seek out this kingdom of His and His righteousness. This was when I let the search begin!

Questions to Ponder

What does living a Christian lifestyle mean to you?

How can you strengthen your relationship with God?

Do you believe that God created you for His purposes?

Are you willing to let go of things that will hinder your progress?

Do you have a mentor and are you under a Godly covering?

When you weep

You have expressed deep sorrow with your tears
From what's been taking place over the years
So many ask and wonder when it will end
Know that I'm here and I'm listening to you friend

The enemy has come in and brought about this pain
But I am greater and will use this for a mighty change
To draw those who will bring about a massive harvest
What the enemy has caused will result for My gain

And know that your weeping has reached My heart
I have seen them and heard your cries from afar
Watch and see Me move mighty on the behalf of all
Because of your weeping many have answered My call

Continue on to seek My will for the nations
And I will pour out an abundance of revelation
That you will rise up and bring My kingdom on earth
Until then, I want you to know I feel your hurt—
When you weep

Letter Six

Hard Times

Balancing parenting and ministry was challenging at times. I was sold out to God. I became dedicated to raising my children in a godly home. I didn't date or have any relationships with men. I was just focused on living my life as a woman of God. As I'm sitting here typing (in 2009) I wish I could be talking about this topic of single parenting on the better side of things. At the moment I am eating peanut butter and crackers because it's one of the few things in my pantry. While I do have financial struggles, I believe I can still minister to you on my level of accomplishments as a single parent. I've been taught that when we start living for God, we immediately become a threat to the enemy. I've experienced many ups and downs financially, but I don't remember it being so stressful to make ends meet before I decided to live for Christ and to follow His teachings.

Yes, it has always been difficult to pay the bills and to keep food in the house, but it never bothered me the way it does right now. I think it's because I'm totally aware of His promises and I want them for both me and my children. Grace, God has never forsaken us. He has been my source and provider and always will be. There are so many times that God has shown Himself as a provider to me because He is a faithful God.

Thinking back to a few years ago, I was in need of some body soap. In a house of five, soap seems to melt away very quickly. I didn't have enough money to purchase soap at all, but we had to take baths so there I was looking through purses to find enough money to buy the soap. I went to the store and looked down the aisles, and when I saw that the prices of the soaps didn't come anywhere near to matching what I had on me, I became sad. My favorite bar of soap is the pink Dove. I was about a dollar and some change short of having enough to buy it so I got the cheapest one I could afford.

This really shook my faith. I mean, here I am a child of God, trying to live according to His commandments, standing firm on His Word and His covenants, but can't even afford to buy my favorite soap. I had drifted into the trap of paying attention to my circumstances and not focusing on the promises of God. One scripture that came to mind was, "If you remain in me and my words remain in you, ask whatever you wish, and it will be given you" (John 15:7 NIV). Even Dove soap!

When I got home that evening I was very sincere with God in our communication. I told Him that my heart was sad because I wanted to bathe with some pink Dove soap. At that moment, I would have been pleased with just having something that was a pleasure to me. Plus, there is nothing more soothing than a hot bath with your favorite soap! So I went on with my night, and a few days later a friend from church told me that she had something for me. I met with her and she handed me the unthinkable. The Lord had put it on her heart to bless me, and in that package was a pack of Dove soap! I was totally amazed. God was watching over me and listening to my silly little conversation about wanting the soap—and He gave it to me.

This is the kind of thing that He does quite often. It's such a pleasure to know that He hears me. There were other events where God really showed me favor in my times of need. I had a utility bill that was due for a cut-off. When I received the notice about a week before it was scheduled to be cut off, I didn't have the money to pay the amount due. I had been getting some child support but not enough to cover the cost of living comfortably. In other words, my ex-husband paid what he wanted whenever he wanted. My lights were about to be turned off, and I started to panic. I didn't know what I was going to tell my children. How could I explain to them that I'd failed as a parent and they were going to have to suffer from that?

When I called the utility company I was told they were in route to shut my utilities off. I felt that God was trying to communicate to me in a special way so I called again. After the people I spoke to told me the same thing twice, I called again. It's interesting how I kept getting the same answer but felt something would change. During the third call I was told that the cut-off notice had been canceled. Glory be to God! I couldn't believe what I was hearing. I was so excited to see how God once again came to my rescue in an extreme need. He is truly faithful, Grace. There were a couple of times since then when I couldn't pay the utility bills, but God still granted me favor and grace. Instead of the company turning my power off completely, they would just send someone out to turn the gas off. One time my gas was off for two weeks because I didn't have the money to pay my utility bill. I had to boil water for us to take baths! Grace, I don't like bathing in cold water, so it wasn't a great feeling at all.

Raising four children isn't the easiest thing when you want to have a personal life as well. I have sacrificed a lot of my desires so that I could focus on my children and give them the best life I knew how. As of the writing of this book, I have abstained from sex for seven years. I can't even begin to explain the pain of loneliness and the extreme desires to feel loved by a man. The problem with waiting all these years for God to send the man He has for me is that I haven't been happily waiting in expectation. I didn't like celibacy or even the thought of it, but I made a choice to glorify God with my lifestyle and I wanted to be a great example for my children. Honestly, I don't like being a single parent.

This thought reminds me of a time about six years ago when I was at church and one of the associate pastors asked me to lead a single parents ministry. I was so against the idea because I wasn't happy in my singleness. Yes, I was a great parent and raising my children in a Christian home, but singleness wasn't my favorite state of living at the time. God had to heal my heart more and fill the voids that were so deep within me. Who was I to lead a group of people in an area where I wasn't healed or complete?

Things did get better as God promised. I was maturing and my mindset was changing. I was prioritizing and evaluating my life. So I decided it was time for me to stop renting that house from the judge's secretary and purchase my own. It's funny thinking back because my income never really increased. I had a second job a couple of times over the years to help, but it didn't pay much. It didn't matter much to me though because I wanted more space, and besides my son was almost seven years old by that time and still sharing the bedroom with his twin sister. I have three daughters and a son, and my son had begun talking about the need to have his own room.

So I applied for a mortgage loan and found out that I needed to pay some unpaid bills that went back as far as from when I was married. My credit score and report were absolutely ridiculous. I made some settlements and sacrificed a lot to pay off some of the accounts. I also opened up a credit card account to help with my credit score. I worked hard to reestablish a good payment history so I could get the approval I needed from the financial institutions. A couple of years went by and I reached my goal of establishing a good and improved credit score. I resubmitted an application for a mortgage loan and was approved! I was extremely excited and felt great. I thought this would be a great start to a new beginning of purchasing my own home. There is nothing like having your own (husband and all).

Somewhere during the process of the approval, and after I found the house I wanted to purchase, I was informed that I would need about three thousand dollars to close on my home. I didn't have that kind of money and didn't know what I was going to do. Around that same time my grandmother got a big settlement from her property, and she told me that she would help out. Very confident of this, I turned in a notice to my landlord and started packing. My landlord found another family to rent the house, contracts were signed, and I was excited to know that I was on my way to homeownership.

Grace, the events that occurred after this were the most challenging of my faith. My grandmother decided not to give me the money about a week before my closing date. My real estate agent tried everything she knew to get me in that house. The sellers even offered to lease it to me for a year until I was able to purchase it, but the rent would have been five hundred dollars more than what I was already paying. I knew I wouldn't have been able to make ends meet, and I also knew I couldn't take that offer because I didn't have the deposit or the first month's rent.

The week before I was scheduled to move out, I went out of town for ministry training. My mom was really good about helping me purchase the tickets to travel when needed. I was taking online courses from Christian International and was required to travel there for some of the Apostolic and Prophetic Training Modules. Although I had to travel, I was very concerned about what I would do once I returned. Completely hopeless, I went away not knowing how God would help me with this one. He had proven His faithfulness to me over the years, but I couldn't tap into my faith concerning this set of circumstances for nothing.

Before I left Florida, my agent told me she had found a house I could lease that was more affordable. I finally felt like I was going to make it through what seemed to be a nightmare, but later I found out the house wasn't available. When I got home I looked around the house and saw packed boxes everywhere. My mom was staying with my children while I was away and finished packing up our things. Sorrow filled my heart as I wondered what to do next. I couldn't live with my mom because she had a house full already: my brother, one of his friends, my stepsister and her children, three dogs, and my mom. I couldn't see how the five of us could stay there too.

My landlord graciously allowed us to stay another three days but was very clear that the next family was due to move in and we had to move out in order to have all repairs made in time for them to move in.

Thoughts of failure flowed through my mind. I felt as if I failed my children, and I couldn't face them anymore. I cried and was miserable. I couldn't believe I was experiencing something so difficult and couldn't understand why I was going through this. I wanted to disappear but didn't know how to make that happen. I wasn't going to end my life, but for that moment I felt I needed a prayer that would suddenly make it all go away. Grace, I don't think I ever found that specific prayer, but God was still leading me.

I called one of my best girlfriends, told her all about my circumstances, and asked if I could store some of my things inside her garage. She lived out of town but had a home in Memphis that was used for vacations and holidays. She told me I could store whatever I needed and more and that we could also stay there as long as we needed. I put most of our furniture in storage and stayed at her house until I found another place to live. We were there for about three weeks before I was able to rent another home.

During that time before I found another home to rent, I was very humbled. I cried a lot and prayed even more. I remember lying on the floor in her bathroom crying my heart out to God and asking Him to have mercy on me. I read Scripture and meditated on God's promises. I prayed and cried some more. I was just pitiful. I saw myself as one who was homeless because I didn't have a place to call home. My friend's house was very nice and furnished. It was nicer than any house I've ever had. The children didn't seem to be affected by things as much as I was, which was very good for me, but I knew I had to find a home for us. I drove around in my former neighborhood and saw a house for rent. Grace, within twenty-four hours I had found a house, paid the deposit, and received my keys!

I don't know why God didn't want me to live in the house that I couldn't finance, but I do know that when we find the place where God wants us to be everything falls into alignment. God revealed to me that I wasn't homeless, I was just in transition. Whether it's a house or a church home you are looking for, when you find that place, God will grant you favor in that safe place.

I leased that house for a year and decided to try again. I never gave up on my dream to purchase a home. I never gave up on believing for God's promises. Sure enough I was approved for a mortgage loan and was able to purchase my first home with the help of my cousin's financial assistance. God had people in place to help me during that process, and it was evident that He was on my side despite the obstacles still coming my way. The day I picked up the keys to my new home, the transmission went out on my car! My goodness, Grace, I was devastated. I was screaming in the middle of rush-hour traffic, "God, why is this happening to me!" My daughter was laughing the whole time. Soon after I purchased a vehicle and was on my way to living out more promises.

One of God's promises to me was that if I would seek His kingdom and His righteousness, all the things I had need of would be added to me. Grace, after all this seeking of God's kingdom, I found out that the kingdom of God had been available to me and within my grasp. His kingdom was in my heart, and when I allowed Him to have full reign in my life I was able to experience peace and joy in the Holy Ghost.

Questions to Ponder

Do you find it difficult to walk by Faith?

Will your faith carry you through hard times?

What kind of spiritual disciplines will you apply to help you?

Can you trust God to provide for you?

Has your prayer life increased at this point of your life?

Beautiful One

Beautiful One is what I would call You
Beautiful to the sight of my eyes
There aren't words known to me that even describe
How precious is this One that lives inside

In the depth of my soul rests a willingness to please You
Every thought of You brings about a gentle smile
My eyes are enlightened when I think of this truth
My spirit is on guard waiting for Your commands

The song of the Lord springs forth as I adore You
My expectations of Your perfection are great
As I sit before You with childlike faith
I even know that every concern is in Your hands

Beautiful One is what I would call You
Beautiful to the sight of my eyes
There aren't words known to me that even describe
How precious is this One that lives inside

I hear You ask "can you keep a secret?"
In anticipation of what You have to share
I bring my ears in attention to hear
but soon discover You're not there

What is this game of hide and seek?
I don't want to be away from You any longer

I call out to You now dear come to me
Your appearance satisfies my hunger

Beautiful One is what I would call You
Beautiful to the sight of my eyes
There aren't words known to me that even describe
How precious is this One that lives inside

I have now entered into a place
Where I know Your Spirit resides

Letter Seven

Final Words to Single Parents

Grace, as I look back to my first letter to you and think about all the things God has brought me through, I can truly say that I've come a long way. I've been delivered from a lifestyle of sinfulness and can attest to you that God is faithful! I've told you before that it's not an easy road to travel at times, but there is a Helper who will be there for you every step of the way. My testimony of the goodness of God grows daily, and I am grateful for every ounce of His grace along the way.

I would not have made it this far without prayer. Talking to God has kept me in peace during the most difficult times of my life after the divorce. The more I shared my fears and concerns with God the more He turned things around in my favor, and my faith grew.

God has sent many people my way to bless me. They would say that God placed it on their hearts to give money, clothes, food, and even a car. God continually shows me that He hasn't forgotten about me and my babies. He is and always will be my source of provision. When times got hard I could always depend on God to make a way for my family. I also then had more faith to believe for His provision in the lives of others.

Just a couple of weeks ago I was at church enjoying our Bible study, and someone asked me to pray for a young lady who was in the hall crying loudly and yelling on the phone. By the time I was able to get to her she was sitting on the floor crying and telling the person on the phone that she was tired. She said she wanted to give up and would rather be dead. I gently asked if I could pray for her. She yelled, "What can prayer do for me now!" She said she wanted to be dead. She then got off the phone and I began to pray.

I held her as she sat on the floor and prayed for her. She told me she had five children and was in an abusive relationship and wasn't receiving much support for the children. At that very moment, I saw my past from a far distance and knew that I had to finish my letters to you. I wanted you and others to know that prayer works and that God can intervene in any situation to bring help. All you have to do is call on His name and He will come to your aid. We can have peace in knowing that God will answer our prayers.

Grace, I want to share with you more about the loneliness of a single parent. Do you remember my testimony of how I was so sexually bound after I divorced my ex-husband? I was very lonely inside and thought someone could fill a void that was only intended for God's Spirit. I was a very sensual person and was quite in tune with stimulating my body. Well, Grace, after several years of celibacy and dedicating my life to the work of ministry, I would often drift back to that state of mind. Sometimes I got tired of waiting on God to present me to the man He has for me, and thoughts of compromise would spring forth. I found myself wondering what my life would be like if I settled for a mate for companionship or to fill fleshly desires. After praying about it, God would deposit wisdom inside of me and remind me through His Word why I exist and why I am striving to live a lifestyle that is pleasing to Him.

I would then go to war and start quoting the Word of God so that my mind would be renewed and I could get back on the road of purpose and fulfilling my destiny. What I can offer as encouragement if you find yourself in this place is first of all to know that feelings of loneliness will happen. But one thing I know for sure is that I would rather be on this end of the road than the beginning of my singleness. Before, I had men sleeping with me and I felt as empty as an abandoned coke bottle on the side of the road. I had men "loving" on me, but because they didn't belong to me they had to leave. Those were just moments of temporary gratification. Temporary gratification only makes a deeper hole for loneliness.

God desires us to be whole and complete. That wholeness can only be experienced through the love that Christ ordains. Whether it's with the spouse that God gives or just through the joy that comes from His Spirit inside of you, you can be complete in Christ. There is much more peace in my home today although I still want a spouse. And, to tell you the truth, after listening to all the drama from friends about relationships gone wrong, I am glad to be in this place with God.

Thoughts will go through your mind saying, "Just do what everyone else is doing... nobody's perfect." You will even find yourself thinking, "If she has someone, surely I could have someone in my life." Discouragement will knock on the door to your heart, and you will find yourself feeling as though you've failed or missed your opportunity to be with the love that's intended for you. Thoughts of

"I'm so unattractive now and I'm getting older" will usually find their way into your head as well. These are some of the thoughts I've had to conquer, and if the truth be told, you are in the best position to be blessed by God if you can relate to this.

It's during those times of feeling empty when God is able to show Himself strong in your life. When I allowed God to fill those areas of void or lack, I saw myself differently. I wanted God's love and acceptance more than a short-lived fling. Yes, there were areas where I needed healing from past relationships, emotional imbalances, insecurities, and even selfishness. Honestly, Grace, I still deal with emotional imbalances! God is not finished with His work in me for sure.

I came to the realization that no matter what I can get or have, it can't replace the love of God that's in my heart. Nothing material will do it, and no temporary physical supply can fill it. Fall in love with God, Grace. Let Him show you what you're really worth. It's a miracle that I have been able to abstain from sexual activities for over seven years considering how bound I was in this sin. When desires of wanting to be intimate with a man came upon me, I would pray, fast, and ask God to remove those desires until the proper timing of being joined with the husband He has prepared for me. It's a miracle that I am in my rightful mind from all the battles I've been through.

I've learned to endure and wait through all of this. Waiting isn't the easiest thing to do, but I believe that as you wait on that special person to enter your life, you will also be learning more about yourself—the real you. I've fallen in love with God through waiting and allowing Him to teach me more about being close to Him. Grace, know that there is hope and there are people who care. Even better, God cares about you. He has you in this world for His perfect plan.

When times get rough, share your frustrations with others. It always helps to talk things out. I was having a really bad day and decided to write the president of the United States of America. Yeah, that's me, so fed up with my circumstances that I was going to tell someone about my frustrations. I wanted the president to know that there are people like me out here waiting on a change. I wanted him to understand my pain so I decided to have a heart-to-heart moment. Below is my letter to President Obama along with a correspondence from the White House:

Mr. President,

> I wanted to take the time out to share some of the things that are on my heart. I am a 35-year-old single parent of four. I am very dedicated in taking care of my responsibilities as a mother and provide a caring environment for my children. I have decent employment, well I suppose if you compare it to those who don't have much at all.
>
> I'm having financial challenges that are very stressful at times. I am placed in a bracket in which I earn too much income ($34,000 annually) to get assistance and barely have enough to make ends meet. I've sacrificed a lot to place my children and myself in a good neighborhood where we feel safe and secure. I've worked two jobs at times since my divorce nine years ago and have considered doing it again. My ex-husband is "self-employed" and it's very hard to prove his income in an effort to

receive the amount of support I deserve. I agreed on $800 a month for four children about nine years ago, and that's what he is ordered to pay as of today. In addition, there are times when he "helps" a little more by giving directly to them. This is not about making one parent seem to be less than the other, but I just want to share my life with you...for what it's worth.

I've been employed with the Shelby County Government for 15 years. I've applied for several higher paying jobs but with no success. I consider myself as one who aspires to great dreams but have had many obstacles and hindrances in life. I am a person of very strong faith and I know that even if you never receive this letter, God hears me and knows my struggle and will answer my prayers.

With all of the responsibilities you have as President of the United States, I still expect you to at least read my letter. I mean if God hears the entire world then surely man (especially one who He has allowed in such office) could take the time out for...just me.

Mr. President, how are you going to help heal this world of financial distress and woes? I know you stepped into a big mess of an ordeal, but do you have a plan that would affect someone like me? And why doesn't the government pay the employees more than what we receive? Shouldn't there have been a stimulus bill that would have at least given government employers the ability to expand their budgets? Instead of just helping automakers? I understand there is help for moms who may want to continue their education, but realistically, are the jobs available?

I can't help but ask God at times, "Lord, am I ever going to get ahead?" Do you think the world's system of doing things could be changed? Our nation shouldn't be in borderline poverty, and of course so much is to blame, but little is available as a solution. Medical insurance has risen; the cost of living goes up, but with no increase of pay.

I'm sure you hear the cry of a nation's tears. I couldn't imagine the warfare and concerns you must have on your shoulders as the leader of our nation. I also believe that if the proper people are appointed to be liaisons over the concerns of people like myself, change could be implemented.

So for someone like myself, a single parent of four who makes about $34,000 annually, who tries to live an honest life but can't get any assistance, who is behind on bills and has been turned down on promotion opportunities, and is trying to provide a close to normal life for my children...what can the President of the United States offer as encouragement?

Temiika Gipson

Dear Temiika Gipson:

Thank you for taking the time to write and share your personal experiences.

I am working diligently every day to address the hardships that many people like you are facing. Far too many hard-working Americans are struggling—falling behind on mortgage or rent payments, losing a job without warning, or shouldering crushing medical bills while coping with illness.

Each day, I read letters from the millions of Americans who write to me so that I remain connected to the real-life challenges of families across the country. It took many years to create our Nation's current challenges, and it will take time to bring the change that our families need.

We have already begun building a solid foundation to help overcome the real struggles that Americans experience each day. The investments we are now making will create or save millions of jobs, fund much-needed reforms in our health care and education systems, and help strengthen our communities.

As we work together to improve the lives of all Americans, please know that the trials and triumphs of Americans like yourself motivate my Administration to work even harder to overcome the challenges before us. I am confident that we will come out of these tough economic times stronger than before and with a renewed promise of a better future for all in our Nation.

Information on jobs, health benefits, housing assistance, and other public resources available to those in need can be found by calling 1-(800)-FEDINFO or by visiting: www.usa.gov. Thank you again for writing.

Sincerely,
Barack Obama

After receiving the correspondence I thought, wow, he really cares, and I was definitely encouraged. I believe God is going to turn a lot of things around for our nation. I have enough faith that God will continuously watch over His children. With our obedience, we will receive His promises.

A Prayer for Single Parents

Heavenly Father, I honor You as Lord and Savior, and I thank You for who You are in the lives of those who are reading this prayer. I thank You for breaking the walls and barriers that have kept them from Your love and from Your fellowship. I thank You for drawing each person closer to You as their hearts and minds are opened to receive You.

I ask that You will allow Your presence to fill the very space in which they are in. Dear Lord, I release the anointing of God to fall upon Your child. And with that anointing I ask that it would penetrate through the thickness of sin, the sickness of their bodies, and the bondages formed from life situations. Break the yoke of the enemy with Your anointing! I release the blood of Jesus over every reader and decree that they are set free from rejection, rebellion, depression, and the like. I release a breaker anointing and consuming fire upon them that will deliver them from that which has kept them bound even generationally, and I decree and declare that they are delivered and set free.

I decree and declare that they are healed from all traumatic experiences that have caused emotional wounds. I decree and declare that they are healed from being in abusive relationships. I decree and declare that they are healed from mental disorders caused by abandonment and alienation. I decree and declare that they are healed from sicknesses that were caused from harboring unforgiveness.

Father God, be their Sanctifier. Be their Righteousness. Be their Peace. Be their Advocate. Be their Bread of Life. Be their Comforter. Be their Chief Shepherd. Be their Counselor. Be their Foundation. Be their Friend. Be their Guide. Be their Mediator and be their Way.

I thank You for providing for every single parent. I thank You for releasing the funds needed to care for their families. I thank You for watching over their children and making sure they are safe from evil and harm. I thank You for shielding them with Your protective arms every day and throughout the nights. I thank You for placing Your choice of people in their lives to fill in where a parent is lacking or missing.

I give all honor and praises to You for intervening in their lives today! It's in Jesus' name I pray, amen and amen!

Dear Grace, this is my testimony of my experiences after I accepted my call to ministry…to be continued.

About the Author

Temiika D. Gipson was born on December 11, 1973, in Memphis, Tennessee. She is an ordained minister of the gospel and founder of Repairer of the Breach, an online international ministry in which she prophetically releases the voice of God through her writings.

Temiika is called in the office of a prophet and has received a host of apostolic and advanced prophetic ministry training certifications. She is also a certified instructor with Christian International Ministries Network for their *Ministering Spiritual Gifts* manual and has a Bachelor of Ministry degree from International College of Ministry.

Temiika is very keen on hearing from God by His Spirit and operating in the gift of discerning of spirits. She functions as a minister and prophetic intercessor at New Direction Christian Church where she is dedicated to serving God and equipping others in the prophetic ministry and intercessory prayer. She also is very skilled in the area of spiritual warfare training.

Temiika is the mother of four beautiful children.

Contact Information

Repairer of the Breach Intl Ministries

Temiika D. Gipson

P.O. Box 3011

Cordova, TN 38088

deargraceletters@gmail.com

www.TemiikaGipson.org

~Notes~

~Notes~

~Notes~

www.ingramcontent.com/pod-product-compliance
Lightning Source LLC
Chambersburg PA
CBHW031654040426
42453CB00006B/309